Seaton, Axminster & Lyme Regis

IN OLD PHOTOGRAPHS

Dr Edward Tonge and his father outside Shepherds Cottage, Beer. A native of Yorkshire, Dr Tonge came to the Beer practice in 1897, where he remained until his death in 1937. He took a keen and practical interest in the affairs of the village, giving help and encouragement wherever needed, never sparing himself in the cause of others. He lived for his work and, faithful to his self-imposed duty, he left his own sick-bed to minister to those whose needs were greater. This great care that he gave to the people of Beer endeared him to everyone. His name became synonymous with Beer and when he died, aged 64, the entire community mourned him. During the First World War he was Principal Medical Officer in charge of the Seaton Auxiliary Hospital, sited at Ryalls Court; he also acted as an Admiralty surgeon. For that work, Dr Tongue was awarded the OBE.

Seaton, Axminster & Lyme Regis

IN OLD PHOTOGRAPHS

Collected by TED GOSLING

Alan Sutton Publishing Limited
Phoenix Mill · Far Thrupp
Stroud · Gloucestershire

First published 1992

Copyright © Ted Gosling

Dedicated to the photographers past and present, professional and amateur who made this book possible.

British Library Cataloguing in Publication Data

Gosling, Ted
  Seaton, Axminster and Lyme Regis in Old
  Photographs
  I. Title
  942.35
ISBN 0-7509-0102-0

Typeset in 9/10 Sabon.
Typesetting and origination by
Alan Sutton Publishing.
Printed in Great Britain by
WBC Print Ltd, Bridgend.

Contents

	Introduction	7
1.	The Towns	9
2.	The Villages	53
3.	The People	65
4.	High Days and Events	91
5.	Rousdon and the Landslip	119
6.	Transport	131
7.	Sportsmen and Sporting Events	143
	Acknowledgements	160

The Ship Inn, Axmouth, *c.* 1935. The landlord of the Ship Inn from 1926 until 1953 was William Worden, pictured here with family members outside his pub. Left to right: Miss Peggy Worden, Mr Eric Worden, Mrs W. Worden (landlady), Miss Eileen Worden, Mr William Worden, Douglas Worden. William was a big-boned giant of a man. An ex-policeman, he would settle any trouble in his pub by picking up the culprit and throwing him into the nearby brook. Another important job he undertook in the village was the butchering of pigs. Before the Second World War, most people kept a pig. Worden butchered them in the skittle alley of his pub. They always squealed when William arrived wearing his apron with a little sticking knife in his hand. They would do everything to evade capture, but to no avail.

Introduction

I don't know why I was invited to write this introduction nor why, at the time, I accepted. I suppose there was an element of friendship in both, and the acceptance was certainly influenced by my lifelong interest in archaeology and history from which I derive enormous pleasure. I also believe that we should encourage the creation and publishing of books like this for, even today, too many of our historic records are lost.

At all times and all over the world the human race has shown an interest in its past. In historic times, Homer and Thucydides from among the Greeks, and Suetonius and Tacitus from the Romans, are just well known examples from a long list of those who researched and recorded events and people for their contemporaries and the future. Homer lived about 2,800 years ago, so this is a long tradition. Monastic writing and education increased the volume of material, while the advent of printing and bound books helped to create some permanence. Painting, sculpture and other art forms added illustration, so that names became faces, shapes and characters. Without Trajan's column in Rome, we should know a lot less about the armour, equipment, vehicles and ships of the Roman Army.

Like the first step on the moon, photography brought a giant step forward for man in recording history in all its forms, as well as much else. More recently we have acquired television and video recording which have added to this ability. Preservation is essential if any of these things are to record and replay history for those who follow. Certainly much more has been lost than has survived. Consider your own actions: local newspapers and magazines contain a record of our area as it is today; tomorrow it will be history, and yet how many of us who have an interest take the trouble to collect cuttings and photographs for the benefit of our children and later generations?

One wonders just how many local photographs would have survived and been made available to the general public if it were not for people like Ted Gosling who, with interest, determination, application, hard work and sometimes great inconvenience, build up, protect and identify great collections of past photographs of people, places, events and objects – the stuff of local history.

This is Ted's second book on the towns, villages, houses and people of Lyme Bay, its coast and a few miles inland. The first covered the area west of his hometown of Seaton. This one crosses the Axe to Axmouth and goes east. If you have any association with the region you really should collect both volumes, for they are an excellent record of the area as it was.

We tend to think of roads as communications inside and between our towns and villages. In fact, some of the older ones influenced the later siting of those places. The well known Fosse Way, for example, probably starts near Axmouth and heads north near Weycroft Bridge and Perry Street. The Great Ridgeway and the Ackling Dyke were both very important, too, the first to early man and the other to the Roman Second Legion. The Great Ridgeway reaches the area via Raymond's Hill, Trinity Hill, Dowlands and Axmouth, while the Ackling Dyke runs from London to Dorchester and then west to enter Axminster as the Lyme Regis road. Perhaps a little further on it may join the Fosse to run on to Exeter.

Ted's photograph collection shows how parts of these historic roads are still in use to serve our modern needs. He also illustrates buildings of all kinds – houses, cottages, farms and churches – as they were, sometimes beyond living memory. The people, many now gone, are clearly recorded and very recognizable in their schools, at work or at play.

This is not simply nostalgia, it is an important contribution to recorded local history.

Norman Whinfrey, 1992

SECTION ONE
The Towns

House above the Great House, Broad Street, Lyme Regis, 1924. At this time this little shop was a greengrocer, and a rabbit and poultry merchant. Woolworths is now on the site.

Pound Street, Lyme Regis, *c.* 1880. Pound Street was called St Michael's Street in the Lyme Plan of 1841. Although this picture was marked 1880, the dress of the men with stove-pipe hats suggests an earlier date.

The Buddle, Lyme Regis, *c.* 1907.

Waterfall and old cottages at Uplyme, c. 1875. This view is of great local interest, picturing a part of Uplyme now gone.

The western half of the Lyme Regis Assembly Rooms, c. 1885. The Assembly Rooms stood on the site that is now the Cobb Gate car park. At this time the main part was a Gentleman's Club. The Assembly Rooms were demolished in 1928.

Jericho, Lyme Regis, *c.* 1885. This is an area of Lyme Regis once known as Jericho. Note the distinctively shaped pushchair with three wheels, and the girls' clothes – frilly white aprons to keep their dresses clean, thick woollen stockings and boots. The house in the centre has now gone and the old mill at the rear has been converted into flats.

Silver Street, Lyme Regis, *c.* 1895. The main road from Lyme Regis to Axminster was used by traders, such as Mrs Hoare the poultry woman. She travelled in twice a week from Musbury, via Uplyme, with her donkey and panniers. She sold chickens, ducks, eggs and vegetables. The shop on the left was then occupied by Paul & Sons, glaziers, decorators and picture framers.

The top of Broad Street, Lyme Regis, *c.* 1896. The shop at the top left is a chemists named Thornton's. Opposite on the right is the Volunteer Arms, and the shop below this public house is Dunster's, printer and publisher of many local prints.

Silver Street, Lyme Regis, *c.* 1892. This view is from outside Grove Cottages. How quiet and peaceful it was then, with children deriving entertainment from games in the street.

Broad Street, Lyme Regis, c. 1890. The shop at the bottom right belonged to James Farnham, watchmaker and jeweller, who specialized in fossil jewellery. The New Commercial Hotel next door provided first-class hotel accommodation and was owned by Mr W.G. Cornish. Street lighting was then provided by the Lyme Regis Gas Works.

General View of Lyme Regis, c. 1895.

Picnic at Axmouth Harbour, *c.* 1924. This was a more peaceful place at this time, but the view remains much the same as today.

The Cottage Hotel, Seaton, *c.* 1926. Situated on the seafront and facing south, the Cottage Hotel was run by Mr W.S. Stokes. The hotel was renamed The Bay in 1931 when it came under the management of Mr E.V. and Mrs M.J. Driver. A new wing was opened in May 1939 with a spacious new lounge and a large sun verandah. Unfortunately this hotel was demolished in 1990.

Axmouth Harbour, Seaton, *c.* 1890. Prior to 1850, Squire Hallett, who at that time owned Stedcombe Manor, spent large sums of money in an attempt to improve the life of the estuary. A pier was built, and two schooners with mixed cargoes plied regularly between Axmouth and London. However, just as the seaborne trade was under way, the railway appeared. By the 1890s the harbour was deserted.

Smith Lending Library, Fore Street, Seaton, *c.* 1923. W. Smith, who was a printer, ran a successful lending library and fancy goods shop in Seaton, situated on the present site of Maynews. The library was very popular with the residents, with a stock of over 3,000 volumes. For the children, Smith's had a special library and two showrooms fully stocked with toys. He also ran a similar store in Colyton on the site of the present post office.

View from Fleet Hill on the Colyford Road, Seaton, looking towards Harepath Road, 1974. The fields were once in an area of outstanding natural beauty, but are now covered with large housing estates after an orgy of modernization.

Marine Place, Seaton, *c.* 1963. A roundabout and flowerbeds are being constructed in the centre of Marine Place. The car in the background shows that vehicles could turn left or right at the top of Harbour Road.

Harbour Road, Seaton, *c.* 1921. Formerly Station Road, and one of the main roads into Seaton, this view of Harbour Road was the first to greet visitors arriving by rail.

Trinity Square, Axminster, *c.* 1906. Trinity Square was constructed after a fire on Trinity Sunday, 1834. This destroyed about thirty houses which formed the north side of a very narrow street, extending from the Bell Hotel to the corner of Castle Street.

Newbery's grocery shop, Lyme Regis, Axminster, *c.* 1924. Typical of the old-fashioned grocers shop, Newbery's was also a bakers and offered a high level of personal service.

Butts Cottage, Lyme Road, Axminster, *c.* 1910. Coming from Dorchester and Bridport, Lyme Road is one of the four principal roads leading to the town. This view shows a thatched property, Butts Cottage, which was demolished in 1923.

Millbrook, Axminster, looking up Chard Road, *c.* 1908.

At the top of Pound Street, Lyme Regis, *c.* 1895.

House in Cobb Road, Lyme Regis, *c.* 1928.

An early view of Lyme Regis. Just right of centre is the cart-track by which goods were taken to and from the harbour.

Marine Parade, Lyme Regis, *c.* 1895. The Marine Parade extended from the corner of Broad Street, by Cobb Gate, in a slight curve for a third of a mile to the Cobb. It was much used by townsfolk and visitors alike who would promenade in their finery.

Market Place, Colyton, c. 1899. Follett Stores, on the left, were grocers and ironmongers. The shop also stocked wines, spirits and beer, and was probably one of the first shops in the area to sell mass-produced items such as cooking pots, nails and screws.

Seaton Regatta Day, 1926. During the 1920s, Seaton Regatta Day was held on the last Tuesday in July and was the most popular event of the year. The house in the background, now occupied by the TSB, was then the Esplanade Hotel, a splendid establishment with delightful sea views.

Lyme Regis, *c.* 1924. In the distance rise the heights of Stonebarrow and Golden Cap.

Bell Cliff, Lyme Regis, 1931. This photograph was taken shortly after the Assembly Rooms were demolished. The house in the background is the Bell Cliff Guest House.

The Cobb, Lyme Regis, *c.* 1860. The great storm of 1817 severely damaged the Cobb. The work of rebuilding the present Cobb began on 19 April 1825 and was completed on 18 November 1826. In the reconstruction, the foundations were laid very deep, more so on the seaward side. The interior was of cowstone, worked and carefully laid with occasional courses of cap-stone. The exterior was of solid Portland cap-stone laid in courses.

The Cobb, Lyme Regis, *c.* 1870.

The River Axe, 1972. At one time the Axe had a much wider estuary and the village of Axmouth (in the background) was a place of considerable importance, possessing no less than fourteen inns. Salt was panned in the surrounding marshes and many attempts have been made over the centuries to repair the haven. Today it is a unique, subtle and very vulnerable landscape, a part of our heritage that should not be destroyed through development. If this happened the loss of wildlife and landscape would be irreplaceable.

Shipping in Axmouth Harbour, c. 1864. The house on the left belonged to the ferryman. The harbour warehouses are standing to the right. These were used to store goods brought into the river by vessels such as those here. The rates of tonnage that applied then meant that every ship carrying ten tons or over paid the sum of 2d per ton. The schedule of cargo charges included items like, 'Cider per hogshead, 8d.'

Seaton Beach, c. 1880. This shingle beach was at this time the domain of the Seaton fishermen, hardy men, full of anecdote, who could tell many a story about the sea, many of them having served in the Navy. Even in 1346–7, Seaton furnished two ships and twenty-five men when there was trouble with the French.

View of Lyme Regis Cobb from the east, *c.* 1867. This is probably after the storm of February 1867.

The Walk, looking north-east from the Cobb, Lyme Regis, *c.* 1850.

The Philpot Museum, Lyme Regis, *c.* 1910. On the left is the entrance to the Guildhall. This building was partially restored to commemorate Queen Victoria's Golden Jubilee in 1887. The open area in front of the entrance used to be called Cogmoile (i.e. prison) Square, and is where the stocks were erected.

Interior of Lyme Regis church, *c.* 1875. Dedicated to St Michael, this church now stands almost on the edge of a crumbling cliff. At this time the vicar of Lyme Regis was Dr Frederick Parry Hodges.

Broad Street, Lyme Regis, c. 1908. The little house on the right was Adams the greengrocer, and Sanders had refreshment rooms further up the street.

The Lynch Walk, Lyme Regis, c. 1907. This roadside walk in Lyme is said to have been named after a Lyme merchant from the fourteenth century.

Aerial view, Seaton, 1972. The large building in the centre is the Regal Cinema, which was demolished in 1974. The row of houses on the side of the cinema, known as Violet Terrace, was pulled down at the same time. The massive developments that took place in the Harepath Road area had not yet taken place, and the fabric of the beautiful countryside surrounding Seaton was as yet untouched. Future generations may consider 1972 as a turning point in the history of the town.

Diamond Jubilee celebrations at The George, Seaton, Tuesday 22 June 1897. The townspeople wondered what it would be possible to do to celebrate the Queen's Diamond Jubilee in a worthy manner. Meetings were held and plans made for the great day. Preparations included street decorations for the town, such as the Triumphal Arch built over Queen Street, shown here.

Looking down Fore Street, Seaton, c. 1900. Louds the Butchers is trading in the same shop as today, and Captain Norrie lived next door in Ingleside, now the dentist's surgery.

Bridge Street, Lyme Regis, *c.* 1849. This calotype of Bridge Street is one of the first photographs of the town. Calotypes were the earliest positive/negative photographs on paper after photogenic drawings, and were an improvement on them. An exposure time of a few minutes was required, hence the statue-like appearance of the people. Calotypes are comparatively rare and are of great documentary value.

Pound Street, Lyme Regis, *c.* 1885.

Seaton Station, June 1914. The first meeting to discuss a railway for Seaton was held in the Pole Arms Hotel on 5 December 1863, and the line was finally opened on 28 July 1869. The original station building here was replaced in the 1930s with a modern one of concrete, in the SR style.

Collier's Drapers Shop, Seaton, *c.* 1907.

Lyme Regis Cobb, beach and hamlet, *c.* 1855. The trackway on the left came from the cement works to the Landing Quay. In the background is Cliff House, which was destroyed in a landslip during the early 1960s.

Seaton Beach, *c.* 1905.

St Michael's parish church, Lyme Regis, *c.* 1895.

Looking up Coombe Street from Bridge Street, Lyme Regis, *c.* 1910.

The house on the corner of Meadow Road where it joins Manor Road, Seaton.

The Chine, Seaton, *c.* 1927. Built in the 1920s on an extension of the West Walk, this proved to be a valuable asset to the town.

The Esplanade, Seaton, looking west, *c.* 1925. At this time it was still safe to cross the roads and to stop and talk. It is hard to imagine the little group gathered around the stationary van doing the same today.

Seaton Hole, *c.* 1895. This path, which went to the Old Beer Road, was called Zions Hill. At that time it was joined by a well-defined promenade which stretched from Seaton. This was washed away during the gales of 1915.

Reginald Ernest Aplin and family members, standing outside their cottage in Seaton, 1901. This thatched property stood next to the old primary school in Fore Street. It has now been demolished. At this time a dairy belonging to W.H. Aplin called the Manor Farm Dairy operated from here.

Seaton's Farm Dairy, 1895. Frank Thomas delivered milk, butter, cream, junkets and new-laid eggs twice daily to all parts of the town from his shop on the corner of Cross Street. After one hundred years the shop is still there.

Bird's eye view of Seaton, c. 1896. Note the absence of any buildings between Trevelyan Road and Beach Road. This land was the subject of a proposed housing development in 1860, when Sir W.C. Trevelyan commissioned Benjamin Woodward, the architect, to design a row of terraced houses facing the sea. The project, which Woodward discussed at length in a series of letters to Lady Trevelyan, came to nothing, which was a pity for the town.

41

Cobb Road, Lyme Regis, *c.* 1925. This road, which was constructed in 1832, has always been unstable, and the fear of subsidence must have caused much worry to owners of property in the vicinity.

Lyme Regis Cottage Hospital, 1904. This hospital was opened in Jubilee year, 1897. For many years Miss Coombes was Matron. She was succeeded by Miss Owen, who remained until the hospital moved to Pound Road. The original hospital, which was in Church Street, is now called The Gables and is used as holiday flats.

Windsor Terrace, Lyme Regis, *c.* 1907.

Upper Broad Street, Lyme Regis, *c.* 1900.

South Street, Axminster, *c*. 1899.

Station Road, Axminster, *c*. 1908. The Western Road, leading from Exeter and Honiton, was then an attractive route into the town centre.

Hillhead, Colyton, *c.* 1900. Behind the stone building in the foreground was a brush factory which manufactured artist's paint brushes. It was owned at this time by Mr Tucker. At the end of the Second World War a set of brushes was sent to Winston Churchill. All of the thatched cottages were later demolished by fire.

Fore Street, Seaton, 1962.

Fore Street, Seaton, c. 1929. On the right is the sign of the Golden Lion, a pub that also provided first-class accommodation for visitors. The proprietor at that time was Mr A.E. Loud, known to all as Lion Loud.

Queen Street, Seaton, c. 1901. The fine, mature copper beech tree shown here became a casualty when the present Manor Court was built. It was a beautiful tree, especially during the summer months, and its disappearance was a great loss to the town.

Leigh Terrace, Seaton, c. 1901.

Lyme Regis Cobb, *c.* 1938. Beer
fishermen Dougie Orley and
Ken Tonge (the local doctor's son)
in *Grey Goose*, Orley's fishing boat
from Beer.

Looking towards the Cobb, Lyme Regis Harbour, 1885.

Trinity Square, Axminster, *c.* 1946. Trinity House was occupied by Hepworths, the chainstore tailors.

Western Road, Axminster, *c.* 1924. Although a few cars had appeared, this main route into the town was still a place of marvellous serenity compared with today.

Northern corner of the Three Cups Hotel, Broad Street, Lyme Regis, c. 1930. The proprietors of the Three Cups at that time were Mr and Mrs W. Lloyd. The hotel had a garage for fifty cars.

Cobb Hamlet, Lyme Regis, 27 August 1926. This house was then the home of Dr Wyatt Wingrave, who retired to Lyme in 1923. Wingrave was an ear, nose and throat specialist from Coventry who, after his retirement, founded the museum at Lyme and became the first curator. The house is now the Harbour Inn.

Bridge Street, Lyme Regis, *c.* 1914.

Broad Street, Lyme Regis, *c.* 1905. The Assembly Rooms, on the right, stood on the present-day site of Cobb Gate car park. Demolished in 1928, they were originally intended to be a place where the better class of resident and visitor would meet for refreshments, dancing and cards.

Chantry Bridge, Colyton, *c.* 1950.

The Walk, Marine Parade, Lyme Regis, *c.* 1875.

The Villages

Combpyne, *c.* 1910. Combpyne, wedged in a hollow, is both charming and timeless. Originally it was the combe where people who bore the name of Pyne lived.

Hunters Lodge, near Axminster, *c.* 1930.

New Inn, Uplyme, *c.* 1935. Finding that Lyme Regis Railway Station was at an inconvenient distance from Uplyme, it was petitioned for a Halt to be built near the New Inn. However, before the scheme could be carried out, the National Bus Company started a bus service, rendering the halt unnecessary.

Pound Hill, Axmouth, *c.* 1925. The ladies standing in the doorway are Elizabeth Cross (right) and Kate Cross, her mother.

Axmouth, *c.* 1955.

The Harbour Inn, Axmouth, *c.* 1936.

Haven Cottage, Axmouth, 1896. This thatched cottage, on the corner of Kemps Lane, was used by the farmworkers of Haven Farm.

Southleigh School, 1928. Back row, left to right: Miss Woolnough (headmistress), Jack Farrant, John Spiller, Tim Farrant, Bill Hawkins, Rex Wakely, Sally Summers (infants mistress). Middle row, left to right: Jim Dare, Lily Warren, Beatty Newbery, Lily Newbery, Ivy Underdown, Dora Pyle, Winsome Gardener, Kathleen Gush, Andrew Henderson. Front row, left to right: Ken Warren, Sidney Henderson, Diana White, Joyce Newbery, Hazel Sweetland, Tony Warren, Percy Warren.

Pupils of Musbury School, *c.* 1929.

Combpyne, *c.* 1912. This village is situated in a beautiful combe four miles east of Seaton and one mile north of Rousdon. It consists of a line of farms and cottages dotted along the road between Rousdon and Musbury.

Interior view of Combpyne church, *c.* 1910. This church is dedicated to St Mary the Virgin and dates from the thirteenth century.

Avondale, Combpyne, *c.* 1900. The horse-drawn cultivator (far left) was used to aerate the soil and kill the weeds. The other machine is a horse rake.

Marlborough Cottage, Combpyne, 1937. This old, thatched, detached cottage with a wealth of oak belonged to the Rousdon Estate. At this time it was occupied by Mr R. Down who worked for the estate. Marlborough Cottage was sold for £283 on Tuesday 14 September 1937, when over 140 lots of freehold property belonging to the Rousdon Estate were auctioned.

Axmouth village, *c.* 1899. It is sad to think that the cottages on the right are gone, to be replaced with a more modern building, yet Axmouth itself still remains a true Devon village where old community spirit is very much alive. It is a village as yet not preoccupied with the 'prettiest village' syndrome, craft and antique shops, hanging flower baskets and manicured cottage gardens. It has avoided a large influx of newcomers and is fortunate in that the ones that have arrived have entered into the community spirit that exists there.

Axmouth village, *c.* 1925. These picturesque thatched cottages are at Pound Hill, Axmouth.

Pear Tree Corner, Colyford, *c*. 1894. The houses and wall on the right were demolished when this corner was improved. At this time the largest landowner in Colyford was John Impey, a Scarborough JP, of Coly House. He was born in Colyton in 1846 and was educated at Marlborough and Queens College, Oxford. He was called to the Bar, Lincolns Inn, in 1877 and was a JP for the county of Devon. He was also a major in the 3rd Battalion, Devon Regiment.

Axmouth village, *c*. 1955.

The Hare and Hounds, Whitford, *c*. 1960. Shortly after, this public house was delicensed. The last landlord was Bill Williams. It is now a private house.

Black Dog Hill, Uplyme, *c*. 1910. The old Black Dog, a thatched building, was the coaching inn of Uplyme, where horses and a carriage could be obtained. It was also the place for one of the traditional ghosts of Lyme, the Black Dog apparition, which appeared behind the inn.

Fore Street, Musbury, c. 1920. The post office is in the background. At this time the postmistress was Mrs Hall. The house on the right with the Hovis sign belonged to Mr Bennett. He was the village baker.

Musbury post office, c. 1905. The village of Musbury lies three miles south of Axminster. The parish register contains the following entry of the baptism of the Duke of Marlborough: 'John, son of Mr Winston Churchill, baptised the 26th day of May 1650.'

The Dack Family, Axmouth, *c*. 1947. Left to right: Ross, Keith, Maxwell, Pat (the only daughter, at the back), Mrs Eileen Dack, Sandy, Bruce.

The gamekeeper's son, Axmouth, *c*. 1917. Alfred John Dack, always known as Tim, was born on 26 March 1907 and came to Axmouth in 1910. The family originated from Norfolk. Tim's father, Robert William, came to the village to be the gamekeeper on the Stedcombe Estate. Tim, a quiet and much respected man, worked at first as a gamekeeper with his father and then in the building trade.

SECTION THREE
The People

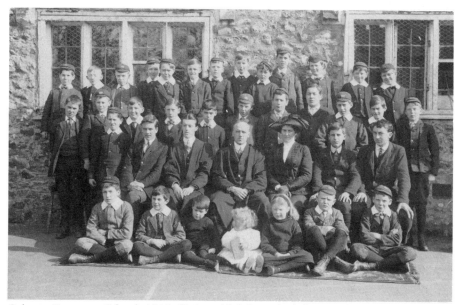

Colyton Grammar School, 1913. Sitting, third from the left, is Lothar Hugo Mermagen, headmaster from 1905 to 1913. He left shortly after to take a position as Head of Ilminster Grammar School. On his left is Mrs Mermagen, and on his right is Mr W.J. Carl, the assistant master. The three children in the middle in front are Mr Mermagen's children. Shortly after this, girls were admitted to Colyton Grammar School after three centuries of male dominance. This, along with the advent of better education for children, put a heavy burden on the premises in the School House in Colyton Square. The number of pupils increased from around forty to over a hundred by the end of the First World War, leading to the move in 1929 to the present site in Colyford.

Apple picking, Thornfield, Seaton, *c.* 1930. Thornfield at this time belonged to Mr E.C. Meade, who also owned many of the neighbouring fields. John Gosling (centre) who is with his sons, Jim and John Junior, worked for Meade as head gardener. He produced all the fruit and vegetables required for the house. Apple picking was always an enjoyable task. Gosling grew many of the old English varieties, such as Lanes Prince Albert, Annie Elizabeth, Lord Derby and the very old local variety called Devonshire Quarrenden. This was a much esteemed autumn apple, superior to all others in productivity, beauty and flavour.

Seaton Beach, 1903. Gwendoline Marsh was a member of a solid, established professional family, her father was a solicitor in Yeovil. Every year the family took their holidays in Seaton, and when they came in 1903 Gwendoline took this enchanting picture of the children of family friend Elsie Howse. The seaside holiday was a special treat for children. They were given the chance to run about in the open air, romp on the beach and experience the delight of a first paddle in the sea.

Seaton Beach, *c.* 1899. A group of young Colyton ladies relaxing on Seaton beach in all their feminine finery. The word MORIDUNUM, in the background, was placed by Joseph Good, the builder, over the south side of the remains of the Napoleonic shore fort. He was following instructions from Sir Walter Trevelyan, who thought Seaton was the site of this post-Roman settlement. The letters were taken down in 1937 when the present toilets were built.

Colyton Fire Brigade, *c.* 1950. Back row, left to right: Bill Bowles, Edgar Smith, George Foxwell, John Copp, Jim Summers, Bert Newton, Harry Potter, George Long. Front row, left to right: Alf Morgan, Percy Turl, -?- (superintendent from Exeter), Bill Long (station officer).

Gerald and John Whatley, *c.* 1930. When they were older, these brothers became members of the 'Eyewell Green and Mooracre Gang'. Their territory ranged from Couchill to Holyford Copse, Black Bridge in the marshes to Blackpool and Three Trees in Big Mead. They were renowned for their expertise with the bow and catapult.

Seaton Hole, 1903. Another holiday snap taken by Gwendoline Marsh. The fisherman rowing the boat was Niper Newton, whose descendants still live in the town, and the lady with the splendid hat is Tibbie, Gwendoline Marsh's sister. Tibbie was a talented violinist and a good tennis player. Sadly, she died of tuberculosis a few years later.

Billy Freeman, Seaton Esplanade, *c.* 1934. Billy was a well loved local character who lived in Stock Lane and worked on the beach until his death in the late 1950s. He sold lobsters, crabs and fish, and was affectionately known as 'Buzzy'.

Seaton fisherman, Joe Eeles, *c.* 1956. Eeles was a member of an old Seaton family. He was born in the town and lived at Leigh Terrace. During the First World War he was a driver attached to the 6th Horse Artillery. He experienced first hand the blood bath of the Front, serving in action on the Somme, at Ypres, Metzwood and Hill 60. Like so many of his generation, Joe Eeles did what he had to do and endured the horrors of trench warfare with a complete dedication to duty.

Albert Samuel Anning, *c.* 1909. Anning was born in Seaton on 3 January 1887 and was a mason for all his working life. A man who took great pride in his job, Anning was also a lieutenant in the old Seaton Fire Brigade when the engine was horse-drawn. The brigade captain at that time was Mr Abbott. Mr Anning is wearing the uniform of the Seaton Territorials in which he served.

Stan Carter, Rousdon, *c.* 1965. Carter, who died in October 1988, was the founder of the Shrubbery Garage, Rousdon. He came from a well known farming family and was born at Rousdon in December 1910.

Royal Observer Corps, Seaton, *c.* 1943. A major part of the town's civilian war effort was carried out by the Observer Corps. Operating from a look-out on Clay Common, they acted as an early warning system and reported all enemy aircraft in the vicinity.

E. Bussell, 1920. Bussell specialized in hand-sewn boot and shoe repairs. Here he is in the doorway of his house in Queen Street, Seaton, opposite the Beer Road junction.

Miss Gulielma Lister, Lyme Regis, 1924.
Lord Lister and his brother Arthur bought
Highcliff in Lyme Regis as a holiday
home in 1870. Gulielma, who was one of
Arthur Lister's seven children, had a
lifelong love for Lyme Regis and compiled
a scrapbook of local interest which is now
in the local museum. Her father, Arthur,
died at Highcliff on 19 July 1908, aged
78. He was a member of an old Quaker
family that had distinguished itself in
science – his elder brother, Lord Lister,
was the founder of antiseptic surgery.
Arthur himself, through his labours on
classes of microscopic fungi, was at that
time the world authority in this line of
research.

Revd Edward Peek, Lyme Regis, c. 1890.
Revd Peek owned and lived at Poulett
House, now the Alexandra Hotel, and
converted the stables of the house into a
place of worship, now the Peek Memorial
Chapel. He started St Michael's College
at Pyne House, Broad Street, and
transferred the school to the old vicarage
in 1888. He also built Coram Tower as a
house for the college masters. The school,
which was intended for the sons of the
clergy, closed twelve months after Peek
died suddenly on 31 December 1898.

Frederick Hawker in his doorway, Guncliff, Lyme Regis, 1924. During his working life, Hawker kept horses, a brake, a double bath chair and a basket chair. Elderly residents were taken for daily drives around Lyme Regis in the double chair to enjoy the sea air. Hawker's father used to ride as postilion for the carriage of the Lion Inn.

Henry Franks Waring of Lyme Regis. Waring built South Cliff in 1842 and lived there for many years. He was Town Clerk in 1836–48. It was he who gave the name to Lucy's Jetty on the walk below South Cliff, where he used to moor a boat of that name. Here he is sitting in a window at South Cliff, shortly before his death.

Harris & Son, Trinity Square, Axminster, c. 1928. Mr Harris and his sons, here standing in the doorway wearing traditional long white aprons, were truly old-fashioned grocers. Their civility and charm are qualities sadly lost in this age of vast supermarkets. The display in the window shows that the store was well-stocked. No doubt as you passed you would have noticed the delicious aroma of coffee, mixed with the smell of the smoked bacon and spices. The boy standing to the right is Lionel Bass.

Abe Newbery (centre) with his father, Isaac (right), 1914. The Newberys were horse and cattle dealers who lived in West House, Axminster.

Mr L. Grant, Axmouth, c. 1956. Ludovic Grant was 'mine host' at the Harbour Inn, Axmouth, 1950–8. He took over the licence from the Beer family who had been landlords for the previous eighty years. Ludo, or 'Mr G.' as he was known, renovated and restored the Harbour. He made an extra bar, 'The Inner Harbour', in the old bowling alley at the rear. He was a great showman and a well loved local character. In the days when pubs didn't serve food, apart from sandwiches and crisps, hundreds of hot pasties were sold at the Harbour during the summer months. These came from the baker in Seaton. 'Mr G.' bought Miss Sanders-Stephens' 1923 Rolls Royce. This was used as an attraction and stood in the car park for several years, until it was found that it was being used as overnight accommodation.

Mr and Mrs Ludovic Grant, Harbour Inn, Axmouth, c. 1956. Pictured here with their son Robin, the Grants were responsible for restarting the ceremony of the Ashen Faggot Burning at Christmas. When the first willow bind burned through, which it did with a large 'snap', the drinks were on the house. Every time the next six went, glasses had to be recharged at the customers' expense. A boar's head was served every New Year's Eve.

Arthur William Collins, Axmouth. Collins was born in Branscombe in 1892 and was married in Axmouth Church in 1922 to Edith Welch. They lived in Branscombe until 1926 when they returned to Axmouth. Arthur became involved in village life, becoming Sexton to St Michael's church. His duties included cleaning the church, tending the oil lamps (the church had no electricity until the 1950s), looking after the boiler during the winter months, tending the church clock, ringing the three bells (one rope in each hand and one rope tied to his foot!) and singing in the church choir. For all these services he was paid the grand sum of £26 per annum. He became a member of the Parish Council in the 1930s and in 1937 became the Parish Clerk. When the First World War broke out he joined the Auxiliary Fire Service. He was one of the founder members of the Axmouth Flower Show, subsequently the Axmouth VPA, whose fifteenth anniversary was in 1992. A commission agent for an insurance company, Collins retired in the 1950s and was a much respected man in the village.

Local photographers, Tony and Mary Byrne-Jones of Seaton, as many will remember them, in their West Walk kiosk. Together they have recorded events during the past forty years. The pictures they have taken will become a valuable contribution to Seaton's history, and future generations will appreciate their work. Most of the pictures in this book were taken by local professional photographers. They recorded events and scenes of local interest that would otherwise have been lost to us. Until recently the value of their work was not recognized, but now a dramatic change has come about and we all appreciate the contribution they have made to local history.

Seaton Home Guard, 1941. Back row, left to right: R. Glen, L. Smith, ? Baker, ? Pritchard, F. Cox, L. Martin, W. Harvey, V. Grieves. Middle row, left to right: R. Holmes, E. Tolman, H. English, T. Tomb, J. Northcott, B. Betteridge, ? Hansford, S. Nicholas, G. Grieves. Front row, left to right: P. Lynch, ? Halford, W. Sutton, T. Terry, L.T. Turner, E. Brown, J. Newberry, W. West. Originally called the Local Defence Volunteers, the Home Guard was a force of armed citizens formed in 1940 for the defence of Great Britain against possible invasion. They were affectionately known as Dads' Army.

William Henry Head of the Wessiters, Seaton, 1894. Head was born in 1874 and was educated at Gonville and Caius College, Cambridge. Here he is (far right) with a group of fellow students. W.H. Head played football, rowed for his college, and was an ardent devotee of hunting, shooting and fishing. He became Seaton's youngest ever town councillor. The Head family had lived in Seaton since 1607 and owned considerable property in the town. W.H. Head, who died in 1958, was the most popular man in Seaton.

Mr and Mrs J Webby, c. 1934. Johnny Webby was the much loved headmaster of Seaton's Sir Walter Trevelyan's School. He was a teacher of outstanding ability and a perfect disciplinarian – when boys were ordered to the front of his class for punishment, they knew they deserved all they would get. The memory of a good man never fades, his influence lives on, and like so many of my fellow Seatonians I am privileged to be one of Johnny Webby's boys.

Uplyme School, *c.* 1960.

Sir Walter Trevelyan Church School, Seaton, *c.* 1910. The teacher standing on the left is Miss Tozer, who remained at the school until her retirement in 1949. Sadly, she was killed by a car while crossing the road on Haldon Hill near Exeter. The man on the right was the headmaster, Mr Oldridge.

Axmouth Village Primary School, 1956. Back row, left to right: Clifton Real, Frankie Beer, Tony Widger, Sandy Dack, Keith Millman. Next row, left to right: Ronnie Real, Keith Legg, Stella Soper, Janet Newbery, Shirley Newbery, Janet Spiller, Carol Widger, Carol Key, Michael Clement, Rodney Morgan. Third row, left to right: Gerald Morgan, Ian Widger, Melvin Millman, Carol Hoare, Monica Clement, Anne Newbery, Frankie Quick, Peter Wright. Front row, left to right: Tim Soper, Clive Millman.

Axmouth Primary School, 1949. Back row, left to right: Pauline Read, Maurine Humphrey, Jean Kaxi, Venna Blackmore, Pat Dack, Rosemary Spiller, Barbara Spiller. Second row, left to right: Terry Pavey, Raymond Puddicombe, Alan Johns, Jennifer Nash, Donald Ostler, Celia Morgan, Ross Dack, Paul Northcott, Albert Snell, Mervyn Legg. Third row, left to right: Bruce Dack, Les Legg, Michael Sweetland, Sandra Key, Jean Johns, Heather Cockram, Gwen Shepherd, Gwen Ostler, Keith Dack, Robin Legg, David Vaughan. Front row, left to right: Maxwell Dack, Keith Nash, Tony Widger, Barry Clarke, Sandy Dack.

John Gosling, *c*. 1886. Gosling, who was born in Colyton in 1866, left school when he was ten years old to work on the building of Rousdon Mansion. He left Colyton at 5.30 a.m. and walked to work every day. In later life he became head gardener at Thornfield, Seaton, and was much in demand as a judge in local flower shows. He was a staunch Plymouth Brother and one of the founders of the Seaton Gospel Hall.

The daughters of Mr William Smith, Christmas 1973. These four Seaton sisters were reunited for the first time since 1918. They were the daughters of the late Mr and Mrs William Smith who once owned the newsagents in Colyton. Left to right: Mrs Etelle Smedley (the eldest, she once ran a toy shop in Queen Street, Seaton), Miss Gladys Smith (a popular local figure), Mrs Joyce MacClean (who married an Australian and emigrated to New South Wales), Mrs Phyllis Adams (who emigrated to Canada). In the summer of 1992, two of the sisters were still alive: Gladys aged 100 and Phyllis aged 99.

Jack Beer, a well known Axmouth character, sitting in his favourite seat at Harbour Inn, Axmouth, *c.* 1955.

B.J.M. Donne, Lyme Regis, July 1927. Donne, who was born in 1831, first came to Lyme Regis in 1841. He was a pupil at the school of George Roberts who was the Lyme Regis historian. The famous portrait of Mary Anning collecting fossils was painted by Donne when he was only eighteen. Here he is 93 years old.

Seaton sub-post office staff, *c.* 1899. Standing on the extreme right is Mr William Miller who was the auxiliary postman. His son, Ernest, is sitting on the left on the hand truck. His other son, Fred, is on the left presenting a telegram to Mrs Florrie Gush. At this time the post office was in Fore Street and the postmistress was Mrs Elizabeth Akerman, seen here standing third from the left. Her husband, the late Henry John Akerman, was the third generation of postmasters from the same family.

Seaton Territorials on parade on the Esplanade, *c.* 1912. The expansion of the volunteer movement at the turn of the century, due to the South African War, led to the formation of this Seaton unit.

Seaton Power Station, *c.* 1927. Expensive though electricity is it is a blessing, bringing as it does light and heat at the turn of a switch. These men were pioneers when the first public electricity supply came to Seaton with the Seaton and District Electric Light Company. The power station was in Homer Lane, Seaton. Left to right: Bill Sutton (who remained with the company after it became SWEB) and Teddy Haslop (who later began his own electricity business).

Haymaking at the Wessiters, Seaton, *c.* 1902. Standing in the middle, dressed in white, is W.H. Head, who owned land and property in Seaton at that time. The gathering and storing of hay played an important part in countryside life, and most of the community gave a hand. The hay was first cut with a horse-drawn mower, then picked up using pitchforks and loaded onto the hay wagon. It was then taken to the farmyard and stacked in ricks. The work was very laborious, yet the workers pictured in haymaking photographs always look happy. Their humour was probably helped by the plentiful supply of cider that was available during the break periods.

Cyril Wanklyn, Overton, Lyme Regis, *c*. 1934. Wanklyn, who died in 1943, was responsible for the methodical inspection, arrangement and interpretation of Lyme's collection of municipal documents. The work commenced in 1921 and he finished his task not long before his death in the autumn of 1943. The documents numbered several thousand and included a copy of the first Court Book which covered the period 1309–28. It is certain that only Wanklyn, with his dedication and scholarly approach, could have produced the final result – a library of eighty well bound volumes. For this achievement the people of Lyme Regis should ever be grateful. For over twenty years, Wanklyn wrote articles for local papers and magazines, and after his death these were published in a book, *Lyme Leaflets*. The book he wrote on the history of Lyme, *Lyme Regis, a Retrospect*, is much sought after today.

Leonard Norman, Town Crier, Lyme Regis, August 1951. Dressed in full regalia, the Town Crier is drawing people's attention by ringing his handbell.

Board of Directors, Axminster Carpets, *c.* 1969. Axminster is associated with the famous carpets which bear its name to the present day. The original manufacturer was Mr Thomas Whitty, a local man, who established a factory there in 1755. The business was carried on until 1835, when the factory was closed and the looms were removed to Wilton. This was a great blow to Axminster, and when Mr Harry Dutfield revived the industry in 1937 he had the support of the whole town. The first carpet was produced that year, the first to be made in Axminster for 102 years. At present the success of Axminsters from Axminster is well known, due to the support of a loyal workforce, under the guiding hand of able directors. Left to right: Mr E. Gill, Mr T.N. Duthers, Mr R. Luff, Mr R.M. Laws, Mr N.A. Humphries, Mr W.H. Dutfield, Mr R.J. Wright, Mr S.J. Dutfield, Mr G. Ayres.

Beer Carnival Queen, 1949. The first post-war carnival in Beer took place in 1949 and the Carnival Queen, here with her attendants, was crowned in the Pioneer Garage. Back row, left to right: Madeleine Smith, Mollie Somers (Carnival Queen), Josephine Griffin. Middle row, left to right: Kathleen Strawbridge, Anthony Wilkins (page boy), Jean Turner. Front row, left to right: Ann Collier, Jacqueline Gigg.

Seaton Carnival, c. 1965. This is the Royal National Lifeboat Institution tableau, with many well known locals on board.

SECTION FOUR
High Days and Events

Declaring the Axe Bridge open, September 1907. This was a day of great rejoicing, particularly for the people of Axmouth. Previously when they travelled to Seaton to do their shopping they had to pay a toll of one penny. The day was declared a public holiday for the locals, and the toll-gate was carried away by the people and burned on the beach.

Coronation celebrations, Colyton, 12 May 1937. The big event this year was the coronation of King George VI. The weather was unkind and the day opened with a cold grey morning, but the enthusiasm of the people of Colyton was in no way dampened. Here, some of them are enjoying the day outside the Old White Hart in Lower Church Street.

Empire Day celebrations, Colyton, *c.* 1910. Before the First World War this was a school holiday and an occasion of much rejoicing. Empire Day was held on Queen Victoria's birthday, 24 May, and originated in commemoration of the assistance given by the Colonies in the Boer War of 1899–1902.

Edward VII coronation celebrations, Beer, 1902. The coronation was an occasion of national rejoicing and a full programme for the event was arranged in Beer. The streets were lavishly decorated and at about midday there was a grand procession. The Beer Naval Reservists, shown here, took part. Throughout the day the local people enjoyed themselves. King Edward was well liked and easily the most popular Prince of Wales to that date. In common with the rest of the country the people of Beer were looking forward to a new era – the Edwardian Age.

Axmouth Flower Show, *c*. 1955. The Flower Show was held behind the Harbour Inn. Left to right: Laura Clements, Mary Broom, Win Sweetland, Jim Cross, Mrs Doble, George Johns, Geoffrey Spiller, Edward Spiller, Mrs Pugh, Bob Pugh.

Axminster Market, *c*. 1890. Old Gage the auctioneer, with the white hat, is conducting a sale of sheep. Farming was then, as now, a busy way of life, and market day was the only time to relax, meet people, exchange news and hear farmers talk about the hard times they were having.

Appeal for recasting and rehanging the bells, Seaton, *c.* 1921. There are six bells in the tower of St Gregory's church, Seaton. Two were added at this time as a memorial to the Seatonians who fell in the First World War. One of these bells was entirely subscribed by the women of Seaton. Of the four old bells, two were cast in about 1430 and the others in 1633 and 1663.

Axmouth Flower Show week, August 1948. These are the Axmouth United AFC committee and ladies. The girl at the side with ribbons in her hair is Nancy Sweetland.

Seaton Fire Brigade, *c.* 1960.

Children's cycling proficiency test, Trevetts car park, *c.* 1960. This car park is now the site of Fosseway Court. At this time the Marwyl Cafe was run by Mr and Mrs W. Woolland. With the Seaton children are PC G. Rodd, Ben Turner, Bob Hoskins, Revd George and Mr Shipton.

Uplyme Fete and Sports, *c.* 1910. The man on the left (straw hat and beard) is Mr Bates who owned the Yawl Mineral Springs factory. This factory started in 1896 at Yawl, and at one time sent mineral waters and lemonade to Exeter. The manufacture of mineral waters stopped after the First World War.

Cannington Viaduct under construction, *c.* 1902. Constructed of concrete, this bridge on the Axminster to Lyme Regis railway is supported by nine piers. Note the 1,000 ft long cableway which spanned the valley and greatly assisted the workmen.

Unveiling ceremony of the Uplyme war memorial, 1921. In every town and village, memorials were erected to men who had made the supreme sacrifice in the First World War. They had given their lives fighting for a cause they believed would bring a happier England and a better world.

Meet of the Cotleigh Hunt, Hunters' Lodge, *c.* 1908.

Mr Gould's staff and friends' coach outing, c. 1929. This group of Seatonians includes Mr J. Gosling, Mr Jack Spurway, Mr Gould, Mr Pengelly, Mr Hutchings and the Misses Needs.

Seaton Choir outing, c. 1930. In the centre is the vicar, Revd Robinson. Front row, left to right: Mr D. Taylor, Mr Good, Mr B. Gillard, Mr Taylor. Others include the driver, Frank Jones, Mr and Mrs Northcott, Mr and Mrs H. Clapp, Mr and Mrs Hoskins, Mr Gould and Mrs D. Newton.

Axminster Dance Club, *c.* 1950. This club used to meet in South Street, in a building now occupied by SWEB. In the centre of the front row is Len Duke who was one of the leading lights.

Bishop Curson's visit to St Gregory's church, Seaton, *c.* 1935. Back row, left to right: Reg Wood, Jack Taylor, Harry Clapp, Ted Gillard, Charlie Northcott, Norman Tolman, Arthur Rogers, Joe Vilven. Second row, left to right: Mrs Mason, Albert Hooper, Mrs Stanley, Geoff Sellers, Tom Clarke, Mr Northcott (churchwarden), Harry Good, Jack Parker, Lionel Collins (cross-bearer), Bishop's Chaplain, Reggie Owen, Hugh Collins, Mr Brown (churchwarden), Cyril Rogers, Tom Wayne, Mr Walton (organist), Mrs Hoskins, Mrs Ham. Third row, left to right: J. Dare, John Loud, Eddie Snell, Revd Taylor, R.S. Robinson (the vicar), Bishop Curson, Revd Hayman, Bobby Bazsley, Derek Fursey, Len Rogers. Front row, left to right: Steve Price, Tony Barr, Bill Miller, Douglas Jackson.

St Mary's church, Axminster, *c.* 1907. This funeral service was for a young man, a member of the Territorial Army, who had drowned in the River Axe.

Trinity Square, Axminster, *c.* 1915. Large numbers of Axminster townspeople turn out to witness these armoured cars pass through Trinity Square during the First World War. There was a great deal of rushing forward on the part of the crowd to wish the boys 'good luck', and everyone felt like shaking them by the hand.

Launching of the *Susan Ashley* lifeboat, Lyme Regis.

The *Susan Ashley* lifeboat, Lyme Regis, *c.* 1902.

Anderton & Rowlands Fair, Seaton, 1904. This is Captain Rowland's travelling bioscope in Seaton, 1904. These were the early days of the cinema, then commonly called 'animated pictures'. All were of short duration – only a few minutes each. The films were on humorous subjects, such as a man chasing his hat blown off by the wind, an old dame catching a bus, a runaway horse and van. There was a very funny one, 'Off for the Holidays', when a family of ten children, with Ma and Pa, get into a cab, which disintegrates after starting. There was also a local one of people coming out of the parish church, and one of the company bathing in Newquay. The films were interspersed with a variety show in which Charles Bruno sang, 'It does not matter, it's only me'. There were two glamorous girls in short skirts – most daring in those days – who also added to the entertainment.

Axminster Market, Trinity Square, c. 1890. Benjamin and John Gage were auctioneers, surveyors, valuers, and house and land agents, who held sales at that time in Axminster Cattle Market. Here they are conducting the sale of Bullmoor Farm.

Queen Victoria's Golden Jubilee, Broad Street, Lyme Regis, 1887. The weather this summer was exceptional, as if to give emphasis to the then-popular term, 'Queen's weather', and no day was more perfect than Jubilee Day, 21 June. There were celebrations throughout the land and the triumphal arch spanning Broad Street was typical of the decorations.

Coronation Day, Axminster, 1937. The big event of 1937 was the coronation of King George VI on 12 May. Here the people of Axminster are pictured celebrating in Trinity Square, with St Mary's parish church in the background.

Higher Axmouth, September 1960. A cloudburst caused severe flooding in the village of Axmouth. The sheep-wash was swept away and the roads suffered much damage.

Axe Vale Meet at Axmouth, *c.* 1935. The motor cycle and sidecar on the left belonged to a Seaton fishmonger who, much to the disgust of the residents, used the brook to wash his fish.

Queen Victoria's Golden Jubilee, Axminster, 1887. A feature of the Golden Jubilee celebrations was the spontaneous way in which the residents decorated their streets. Here the triumphal arch over South Street is under construction.

Wedding group at Chatton Hall, Axminster, *c.* 1918. Although this picture was posed, it is still a good example of social history, showing the clothes worn at that time for this sort of occasion.

Seaton Carnival, *c*. 1948. Seaton ironmongers, Frank Akerman & Co. Ltd, with the tableau they entered for the carnival. In the middle is Mr Puddicombe from Axmouth who worked for the firm for many years.

Seaton Carnival, *c*. 1953. Seaton Youth Club entered a tableau entitled, 'Old Uncle Tom Cobbley and All'. Left to right: Eddie Cockram, David Cockram, Tony Coombes, Stan Pritchard, Fred Cockram, Brian Baker.

Queen Victoria's Diamond Jubilee celebrations, Seaton, 1897. The sixtieth anniversary of the reign of Queen Victoria took place on 22 June 1897, and the festivities demonstrated the love and affection felt by her people. Every town and village in the country held its own procession, its own feast for the poor, and its own sports and firework display. George Barton, the Seaton photographer, assembled all the men in the town on the Burrow for this souvenir photograph. The marquee on the left was used for the celebration lunch and tea.

Handing over the keys of the first completed house in Everest Drive, Seaton, 1953. This was a unique moment in the history of both the town and the country. These men were the first self-build group to complete a house and hand over the keys. This achievement was a credit to the people concerned. Left to right: Frank Statham (secretary), Des Garratt, Perc Bowden, Bert Baker, Frank Davis, Ivan Adams, Eddy Purse, Arthur Adams, Tom Bennett, Alan Hayes, Jim Cockram, Gordon Clements, Jim Bastone, Jim Bryant, Len Northcott, Ken Gould, Ron Pavey (occupier of the first house), Burt Adkins, Richard Perry, Flynton Saxby (treasurer).

Axminster Carnival, 1921. This walking tableau, 'Butting Billy', was a skit on a goat belonging to Mr Caddy who lived at Castle Hill. The goat apparently roamed the streets and, if provoked, would butt people. The man with the striped trousers is Fred Ball the harness maker.

Naming ceremony of the locomotive, *Axminster*, June 1946.

Seaton Youth Club Parade, c. 1952. Leading the Seaton Youth Club Queen to a fete in the cricket field are the old Seaton Scout Band who assembled for this one event. They include Ron Anning, Gerald Gosling, Alan Baker, Don Rodgers, Seymour Martin, Brian Steele, Bill Keates, John Cockram and Pritchard.

Ted Gosling driving Seaton Youth Club Queen, Miss Barbara Newton, and attendant Miss Audrey Kaxi, to the Youth Club fete in the cricket field, 1952. The car he used for this event was a pre-war SS Jaguar, the ancestor of the present-day Jaguar.

Axminster Cattlemarket, Trinity Square, 12 May 1904. The cattlemarket was held in Trinity Square every alternate Thursday and at this time was looked upon as the best in the district. A poultry market was also held every Thursday in the Market House. Dealings in corn were chiefly transacted in the various hotels. In the centre is Mr Charles Snell, the auctioneer. Snell's were land and house agents, auctioneers, surveyors and valuers, and had offices in the Square.

Ben Turner taking over as Chairman of Seaton Urban District Council, *c.* 1965. Left to right: Mr H. Garrod, Mr Tom Summersby, Ben Turner, Mr W. Woolland.

Opening ceremony, Seaton Town Hall, 27 July 1904. The Town Hall, built by Seaton builder Mr G. Richards, soon became the social centre of Seaton and featured, among other attractions, rollerskating. Unfortunately this had to cease owing to damage incurred by the floor.

A picnic at Shute, 17 June 1909. This appears to be a middle-class picnic, one where formality of dress is in contrast to the informal eating and drinking arrangements.

Seaton Autumn Show Committee, c. 1953. The Autumn Show was revived by the Seaton Royal British Legion after the First World War. Left to right: Mr Bastone, Capt. Whippell, Mrs M. Wolstencroft, Mr H. Baylis, Mr J. Cross, Mr W. Hutchings, Mr Bastone, -?-, Mr O. Gear.

The staff of Seaton drapers, Ferris and Prescott, 1964. This group is enjoying a celebration lunch at the Bay Hotel in Seaton. Mr S. Ferris, the owner, is sitting at the head of the table with his wife on the left. Others present include Mr and Mrs W. Nex, Mr and Mrs Powling, and Miss L. Anning. The shop in Queen Street traded successfully for over forty years until the retirement of Mr Ferris in 1974.

Moulding & Sons Annual Dinner, Axminster, c. 1956. The group comprises George Moulding, Fred Moulding, Edgar Moulding, Cecil Moulding and their employees.

Dr Tonge and officials in the committee boat, Beer Regatta, *c.* 1935.

Colyton Carnival, 1927. This smart turn-out belonged to the Devon County Council and the tableau depicted was Uncle Tom Cobbley.

Carriages at Lamberts Castle, 6 April 1909. For over two hundred years a fair and horse races had been held at Lamberts Castle. The event always attracted a large number of spectators and included some of the first families in the county.

Camp of the 1st Devon Yeomanry at Rousdon, 1912. Before the First World War, the Devon Yeomanry trained in the grounds of Rousdon Mansion and held summer camps there.

Rousdon and the Landslip

Landslip Cottage near Lyme Regis, *c.* 1911. This cottage provided refreshments for visitors to the landslip. It is said to have been built from the materials of one of the two cottages that were damaged in the slip of 1837. During the Second World War the cottage was used by the Home Guard.

Landslip Cottage, *c.* 1934. Tea at Landslip Cottage was very popular with visitors before the Second World War, and Mrs Gapper's daughter, Annie (left), would carry out trays laden with tea and cakes to serve in the garden. Annie is talking to Elsie Samways and Sylvia Lyons who were friends from Seaton.

The Devon County Dairy School, Rousdon, *c.* 1937. This school was held in the marble dairy of Rousdon Mansion. The marble furnishings were very cold and in the cheese-making class it was difficult to get the curd to set.

Camp of the Royal 1st Devon Yeomanry, Rousdon, 1912.

Rousdon Estate cricket match, Coronation Day, 9 August 1911. Celebrations at Rousdon for the coronation of Edward VII included a cricket match. Sir Wilfred and Lady Peek and their estate workers attended, including Dan Pearce, Farmer Love, Mr Hardy, Ernest Cleal, Rowland Cleal, Mr Bailey (estate gardener), Mr Cook (Sir Wilfred's coachman), Mrs Hamilton, Mrs Williams and Mr Whitchurch.

Landslip, Rousdon, 9 October 1911. This slip occurred on a portion of the Rousdon Estate. The inhabitants of this cottage had a narrow escape for the event took place soon after midnight. Mr Edwards, the occupier, concluded that as there had been a landslip it would be better to remain indoors until the morning.

The Gapper family at Landslip Cottage, *c.* 1896.

Rousdon Mansion, *c.* 1908. Rousdon was at this time the seat of Sir Wilfred Peek. Here the entire village is assembled to welcome him home with his new bride. Sir Wilfred Peek, known as Bart, was the son of Sir Cuthbert Peek who died in 1901. He was born at Wimbledon House, Surrey, in 1884 and was educated at Eton and Trinity College, Cambridge. He was extra aide-de-camp to Sir Arthur Lawley, Governor of Madras and succeeded his father as 3rd Baronet in 1901. The 1st Baronet, Sir Henry Peek, built Rousdon Mansion at a cost of quarter of a million pounds, which in those days was a vast sum of money. A feature of the mansion, the beautiful marble used for the stairway, came from a ship laden with Sicilian marble that was wrecked on the rocks near Rousdon.

Mr and Mrs Gapper's Golden Wedding celebrations, *c.* 1929. This couple lived at Landslip Cottage near Rousdon, and served cream teas to the many visitors who walked from Lyme and Seaton. The cottage has long gone, but many of the older generation still recall with delight the walk to the landslip, the splendid cream teas and the old-fashioned hospitality shown by the Gapper family.

Rousdon School, 1922. Back row, left to right: Bert Phillips, John Pearcy, Robin Beer, Phillip Samson, Reg Down, Brian Collier, Harold Nicholls. Second row, left to right: Eli Collier, Nora Fursey, Edith Fursey, Rose Fursey, Daisy Summers, Evelyn Samson, Elsie Tolman, Florrie Pearcy, Winnie Giles, Irene Collier. Third row, left to right: -?-, Alma Collier, Gwendoline Hunt, Flossie Collier, Bessie Collier, Phyllis Hunt, Edith Pearcy, Cicily England, ? Sansom. Front row, left to right: Dick England, Albert England, Frank Doble, Maurice Harvey, Cecil Doble, Alan Collier, Henry Hunt.

Rousdon Mansion, 14 September 1937. The mansion, which was completed about 1883, was sold at auction on this day for £29,750. It was built for the late Sir Henry Peek (Bart). Having made a fortune in the grocery trade (Peek of Peek Freans Biscuits), Sir Henry created this house and the village of Rousdon. The house is built of grey flint with Purbeck stone dressings and is in the Queen Anne style. Rousdon Mansion is now the home of Allhallows School.

Rousdon Mansion, 1936. Situated in the west wing, this exceptionally fine marble dairy had an inlaid floor with marble fittings and tiled walls.

Rousdon Farm House, *c.* 1866. This is the ancient farm house that Sir Henry Peek pulled down when he enclosed 250 acres of land and built Rousdon Mansion. Sitting in the doorway is a wonderful old character, Old David Symes, and standing beside him is Young Symes, his son. They farmed at Rousdon when, besides the farm house, there were only two labourers' cottages in the small parish.

The new church at Rousdon, 1877.

Rousdon church, 1874. Sir Henry Peek, at his own cost, built and endowed this church in 1872. It stands on the site of the old parish church, which had fallen into ruins, and was dedicated to St Pancras.

The Estate Office, Rousdon Mansion, 14 September 1937. Buyers from all parts of the country attended the sale of the Rousdon Estate, which was held on this day. The estate was described as one of the beauty spots of England and the sale comprised 145 lots, including the Estate Office.

The school house, cottage and post office, Rousdon, 1937. The school contained three classrooms, a dining room and a large asphalt playground. The school house was occupied by the headmaster, and the adjoining cottage by the district nurse. A single room in the building was used as the village post office. At the sale of the Rousdon Estate this property realized £1,700.

Landslip Cottage, c. 1931, showing the garden where cream teas were served.

Mr and Mrs Gapper, Landslip Cottage, c. 1934.

Landslip, *c.* 1892. The landslip occurred on Christmas Eve 1839, one mile from Rousdon. The cottagers who dwelt on the borders of the cliffs were alarmed by a strange and unaccountable noise resembling the rumbling of thunder. Noticing that the cottage walls were cracking and sinking, they made good their escape. During all of Christmas Day the whole place began to sink gently but with a dreadful persistence, until three-quarters of a mile of cultivated land had crashed down upon the undercliff, carrying with it forty-five acres of arable ground, two cottages and an orchard.

Bindon Manor, Axmouth, *c.* 1902. At present the home of Sir John and Lady Loveridge, Bindon was at one time much larger. Although it was supposed to have been rebuilt in the early part of the fifteenth century, the walls of the central block of the house have been dated to the twelfth century.

SECTION SIX
Transport

National Deposit Friendly Society Outing, Colyton, c. 1929. Back row, left to right: Gladys Hawker (née Board), Mrs Ann Barrett, George William Barrett, Margery Love, Mrs Love, Jethroe Love, Henry Sansom, Kitty Love, Norman Love, Bill Edwards, Floss Copp. Front row, left to right: Rose Barrett, Fred Dart, Eddie Dart, Hubert Rendall, Jackie Boles, Sam Edwards, Phillis Edwards, Elsie Edwards, Mary Ann Edwards, Dick Fox, ? Spurway (driver), Bessie Copp.

Opening Day of the Shrubbery Service Station, Rousdon, 21 April 1955.

Shrubbery Service Station, Rousdon, 14 August 1955. This garage, which was started by Stan Carter, provided a much-needed service to the community and is still operating successfully today.

Clapps Transport, Seaton, 1908. Before the First World War the first daily train left Seaton Station at 7.10 a.m. and the last one arrived at 9.50 p.m. Clapps met all trains, and in those days during the summer season a number of large families with considerable luggage arrived for their holiday, especially during August and September. At the turn of the century there were four bus and coach operators in Seaton using horses, but by 1908 Thomas Clapp had bought up these concerns and had obtained the sole privilege rights for the then L & SW Railway. Here, Thomas Clapp is driving the carriage on the right. He was born in 1852 and died in 1938, and was one of the town's great characters. His personal runabout was a pair of trotting ponies attached to a brilliant-yellow drosky, and his normal attire comprised highly polished brown boots and leggings, black-and-white check breeches, a red waistcoat, a brown Norfolk jacket, and with these he sported white mutton-chop whiskers.

Slaughterhouse, Harepath Road, Seaton, c. 1954. The slaughterhouse was situated where Summersby Close now stands. Ted Gosling is sitting in this large Humber saloon car. Next to this is parked a 1928 four-seater Singer Tourer which he purchased for £3.

Dick Iles, AA patrolman, c. 1935. Dick Iles came from Colyton and joined the AA in the 1930s. He was bicycle patrolman in Torbay and his beat extended from Teignmouth to Kingsteinton. After leaving the AA, Iles returned to Colyton and worked for Trevetts Garage in Seaton for over forty years. He was a noted craftsman: during the war, when motor parts were in short supply, he was one of the few men who could build up exhaust valves with the 'BrightRay' welding process.

Seaton to Beer bus service, *c.* 1914. Sitting in the middle of the bus is Dr E. Tonge, the Beer doctor. The vehicle was nicknamed the 'toast rack' and had no sides or doors. This twenty-seater could attain a speed of 25 m.p.h., although with its solid tyres the ride could be rough and noisy.

Dr Tonge and family in their first motor car, 1912. The first motor cars made their appearance in Beer *c.* 1903. It is believed that the very first belonged to Dr E. Tonge. Left to right: Dr Tonge, Ethel Tonge, Leila Tonge, Kenneth Tonge. The Motor Car Act of 1903 made the registration of cars compulsory, with a speed limit of 20 m.p.h. It is clear from the state of the road that at that speed the car would have left a cloud of dust in its wake.

Hunters Lodge, near Axminster, *c.* 1907. When four-horse coaches ran daily along the London–Exeter road through Axminster, Hunters Lodge Inn was one of the posting stations. Although the first cars had made their appearance by this time, the horse still gave much employment to a large number of people. This two-horse brake was driven by Mr Hodder from Charmouth.

Trevetts Garage, Harbour Road, Seaton, *c.* 1937. Trevetts Garage traded successfully for over sixty years. During that time it gave employment to over one hundred people in the town. Left to right: Ralph Anning (Ralph came from Colyford and died of fever in Africa in the Second World War), Stanley Parker (Axmouth), Alec Parr (Colyford), Horace Clark (foreman, Seaton), Dick Iles (Colyton), Bert Williams (Seaton).

Trevetts Garage, Seaton, *c.* 1939. The showroom of Trevetts Garage is situated on the present site of West Country Fayre. Left to right: Bert Williams (Seaton), Mervin White (Beer), Cyril Tyne (Seaton), Alec Parr (Colyford), Maurice Bagwell (Colyton), Dick Iles (Colyton), Horace Clark (foreman, Seaton).

The engine, *Seaton*, was a Light Pacific of the 'West Country' class. In 1968 the nameplate was presented by British Rail to the Seaton Urban District Council. The council failed to appreciate the great monetary and historical value, and through downright carelessness managed to lose it. Bearing in mind the size, this was a very difficult thing to do!

Clapps Transport, Seaton, *c.* 1912. With the coming of the motor car, Clapps quickly adapted themselves to new ideas, changing from their horse-drawn vehicles to cars. The ornate brass headlamps on this vehicle were fuelled by acetylene, and the spare tyre the car carried was forced over the rim of the wheel in the event of a puncture.

Millbrook, Axminster, *c.* 1924. William Gale and his team of horses are hauling timber. At one time Gale worked on the Pinney Estate.

Axminster Station Approach, 1914. A feature of the early days of the First World War was the commandeering of horses by the War Office. Official buyers were appointed by the government and good prices were given for suitable animals. Farm and business premises were visited and in this way most of the best horses in the district were collected. The horses seen here belonged to the Newbery family and after veterinary examination were to be sent for active service.

Cutting timber at the Wessiters, Seaton, 1904. Mr W. Head and his employees are cutting timber with a large circular saw driven by a steam traction engine. In the background is Wessiters Lodge.

Traction engine at the Wessiters, Seaton, 1904. This engine travelled from the farms to the estates. It had three men in attendance who had to be accommodated at the farm house.

Seaton Junction, *c.* 1962. With the opening of the Seaton branch line on 16 March 1868, the station was first named Colyton Junction. It became Seaton Junction in July 1869.

Old Axminster Station, *c.* 1907. This station opened on 19 July 1860. The building was designed by Sir William Tite. The horse-bus standing at the centre belonged to the George Hotel which was at that time under the personal supervision of the proprietor, Mr F.W. Baker. The hotel omnibus met all trains. Known for high-class cuisine and wines, the George was the oldest established and principal hotel in the town.

Axminster Station, *c.* 1963. Lying to the south-west of the town centre and on the old L & SWR route from Waterloo to Exeter, the station platforms were connected by a covered footbridge.

Combpyne Station, *c.* 1903. This was just after the opening of the Lyme Regis railway. Combpyne Station then had a station master and porter/signalman. With a service of six trains in each direction it must have been an easy life.

SECTION SEVEN

Sportsmen and Sporting Events

Seaton Bowling Club, *c.* 1971. Situated in a sheltered spot in the centre of Seaton, the bowling green is an asset to the town. This green was opened in 1929. Prior to that date the game was played on rinks in Colyford Road. Tom Hilder, captain of Seaton Bowling Club, is throwing up a wood on the opening day of the new season. The ceremonial Silver Jack was sent down by the acting president, Mr W.H. Smith.

Seaton Junior Rugby Team, 1912/13 season.

Beer Miniature Rifle Club, *c*. 1912. These are competitors on the fifty yards range.

Axmouth AFC, 1953/4 season. This team played in the southern section of the Perry Street Intermediate League. Back row, left to right: Reg Hoare (linesman), Basil Pavey, Tommy Morgan, Dennis Morgan, David Newbery, Clive Fox, Douglas Lyne, Arthur Ayres (secretary). Front row, left to right: Michael Powling, Raymond Gush, Fred Newbery, Ronald Board, Edwin Newbery.

Uplyme Cricket Club, c. 1955. Back row, left to right: D. Hallett, -?-, J. Stone, P. Apenaswicz, R. Howarth, A. Larcombe, -?-, J. Leys (umpire). Front row, left to right: -?-, A.R. Mason, Miss J. Mason (the scorekeeper), T. Denham, M. Denham.

Stedcombe Manor, Axmouth, 1912. Mr R.W. Dack, who came to Axmouth from Norfolk, was the gamekeeper on the Stedcombe Estate. Here he is tending to the pheasant eggs. It was the gamekeeper's job to increase the head of game for his master's pleasure. Because the development of driving the pheasants demanded larger stocks of game, his job became much more skilled: a breeder of game as well as a preserver. The eggs of the birds were collected and hatched under farmyard hens in a rearing area. The young birds would then be turned out into the coverts which would be their home until they were shot.

Axminster Football Club, *c.* 1954. Back row, left to right: G. Summers, G. Marsh, E. Cockram, D. Baker, B. Williams, D. le Cocq, P. Palmer, D. Chubb, S. Baker. Front row, left to right: M. Willey, K. Vincent, E. Pomeroy, B. Taylor, D. Horgan.

Axmouth United AFC, 1935/6 season. Playing in the Axe Vale League, this was the team that won the Seaton Hospital Cup. Back row, left to right: J.B. Real, B.A. Billows, K.H. Webber, A. Summers, J.A. Real, H.L. Morgan, F.C. Dack, H.R. Owen (secretary), T.E. Tipper, R.W. Morgan, A.E. Spiller. Middle row, left to right: G.A. Morgan, A.D. Tipper, D.R. Morgan, S.D. Worden, H. Clement, R.J. Cross. Front row, left to right: E.M. Spiller, G.A. Spiller (Captain), A.E. Parker.

Axmouth United Football Club, 1925/6 season. Playing in the Perry Street and District League, Minor South Section, this was the club's second season. Back row, left to right: Bernard Nash, Ron Jones, Jack Purton, John Beasley (goalkeeper), Harry Board, Joe Poole, Mr English. Front row, left to right: Ern Richards, Harold Northcott, Jack Bullock, Oliver Potter.

Axmouth United AFC, 1955/6 season. Back row, left to right: Arthur Ayres (secretary), Grenville Morgan, Raymond Gush, David Newbery, Fred Newbury, John Sweetland, Brian Tidball. Front row, left to right: Paul Northcott, Herbie Sweetland, Peter Sweetland, Keith Millman (mascot), Lewis Newbery, Ted Board.

Axmouth School Football Team, 1937. Back row, left to right: David Newbery, Reg Larcombe, Leonard Potter, Albert Larcombe, Basil Pavey, Victor Critchard. Middle row, left to right: John Sweetland, Peter Sweetland, Stanley Harvey, Grenville Morgan, Douglas Spiller. Front: Derek Ostler.

Axmouth School Football Team, 1922. Back row, left to right: Fred Ayres, Oliver Perry, Joe Poole, Mich Dack, Jack Critchard, Ken Webber. Front row, left to right: Arthur Tipper, Alec Summers, Ivor Real, Tom Morgan, Ken Critchard, Herbie Morgan.

Axe Vale Harriers, *c.* 1905. These hounds were established by Mr John Dashwood Lang of Sidbury, Devon, in 1880, drafts being obtained from My Pynsent Matthew of Rydon House and Mr Churchell Langden of the Seavington Harriers. With kennels at Harcombe near Sidmouth, they provided good sport in the neighbourhood until 1885 when Mr Lang gave up the pack. The hounds were then presented to the county by him. The kennels were removed to Seaton and Mr J. Impey Scarbrough elected Master. At this time he still retained that position. Here he is with huntsman Mr W.H. Head and followers. The pack consisted of sixteen couples of hounds of the old Bager-Pye colour with a standard of about 21 inches.

Seaton Cricket Team, *c.* 1905. Although the origin of the club is lost in the mists of antiquity, it is known that the first pavilion was erected in 1879 and cost £50. It was blown down and rebuilt in 1897 when Dr Pattison was secretary and treasurer. The team here comprised local men, playing in a match against visitors. The players included W. Head, ? Loud, H. Jones, S. Rodgers, Bill Robins and W. Agland.

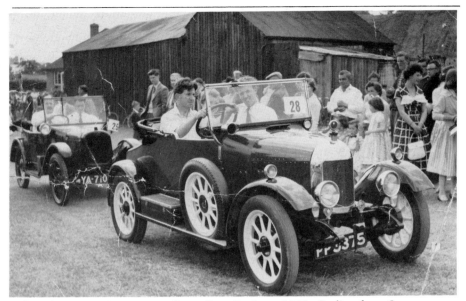

Ted Gosling in a vintage car rally at Bere Regis, *c.* 1958. Gosling from Seaton was a vintage car enthusiast and, although this car needed full restoration, it was purchased for only £5 in 1956. Ted's passenger is Charles Kenlock.

Couchill hill climb, Seaton, *c.* 1936. Counchill was a popular venue for motor cycling events, which included hill climbs and scrambles, from the late 1920s until just after the Second World War. The competitor pictured here is riding a Royal Enfield.

Social event for the men of Rousdon, 1906. This group includes ? Hill, ? Rowe, ? Collins, Jim Gapper, Farmer Love, ? Broomfield, the Rousdon gamekeeper, Greenham (the Bailiff at Charton), Sidney Cleal, Jack French, Jimmy Start (Axmouth), Mike Case and ? Carter. Men like these would spend all their working lives in one village and, although they had a hard life, social events brought relief from the heavy toll.

Rousdon Mansion, 1905. This is a sports day for the Rousdon Estate workers, perhaps a cricket match. The Peeks are sitting in the front with Allen, the family butler, in the middle.

Seaton Cricket Field, *c.* 1903. Fashionable Edwardian visitors are playing tennis on Seaton cricket field. The long building in the distance is R. Dack's workshop in Court Lane. The pavilion (left) stood next to Colyford Road and was demolished before the First World War.

Miniature golf course, Seaton, 1925. Situated on the cliff field, the miniature golf links had two courses of eighteen holes. The charge at that time was 3d per round. Unfortunately this is another amenity that has been lost.

Seaton Football Team, c. 1929. The camaraderie was wonderful in those days, with huge local support for the team. Players here include Fritz Miller, Bert Williams, William Akerman, Nibby Ball and Les Newton. Club officials include Alan Real and Jenks White.

The 'Old Stagers' Team, Seaton Football Club, 1940s. Back row, left to right: Fred Sellers, Cyril Watts, -?-, Ken Tolman, Fritz Miller, -?-, Bill Whatley. Front row, left to right: William Akerman, Ralph Rodgers, Herman Anning, Tom Newton, Harold Rodgers, Fred Osborne.

Seaton Football Team, c. 1952. The Seaton Football Club was formed in 1919 and it has played on the Colyford Road ground ever since. Back row, left to right: Harry Moore, Ron Anning, Bill Keate, Don Rodgers, -?-, Alan Baker. Front row, left to right: Bill Gillard, Horace Critchard, Des Garrett, Len Rodgers, Tony Byrne-Jones.

Seaton Carnival Sports Meeting, c. 1960. Competitors running in the 100 yard event in Seaton football field include Johnny Driver, Les Driver, Arthur Critchard and Des Garrett who appears to be leading the field.

Stedcombe shooting scene, c. 1880. Stedcombe House, Axmouth, stands in a delightful situation among beautiful wooded hills. Squire Hallett, as he was known, was then the Lord of the Manor, and impropriator of the great tithes, the Hallett family having purchased the Axmouth Estate over two hundred years earlier. Mr Hallett died at his London residence on 2 December 1889. The estate then passed to Mr Sanders-Stevens who purchased it in 1891. Left to right: Bob Collins (father of Art Collins, grandfather of John and Wilfred Collins), Major Wills, Col Hallett, Squire Hallett (Stedcombe), Tommy Chapple (Bindon), Bob Palmer.

Seaton Football Team, *c.* 1922. The Seaton Football Club was formed in 1919. Before that date Seaton was a rugby stronghold. The men here were the nucleus of the best team that had played for the club. In the mid-1920s they played in the Perry Street District League and won the Charity Cup twice in three years. Back row, left to right: Joe Collins, Tommy Rodgers, Walt Lovering, Fritz Miller, Ken Tolman, Willy Akerman, Jenks White, -?-. Middle row, left to right: Herman Anning, Les Newton, ? Hoskins. Front row, left to right: Tom Newton, Nippy Ball, Cyril Watts, ? Garland, Ralph Rodgers.

Seaton 'Over 30' Football Team, *c.* 1951. This was a team of much respected and admired local players. Back row, left to right: Wallace Anning, H. Warren, Reg Clarke, Bob Rodgers, Jack Taylor. Front row, left to right: Owen Webber, Bill Woolland, Bunny White, Tommy Beavan, Jim Taylor, Ivor Real.

Meet of the Cotley Harriers, George Hotel, Axminster, 1903. In these days the meet was a wonderful sight to see and the town was a busy and exciting place.

Seaton Bowling Club, *c.* 1962. Members include Percy Litton, Howard Baylis and Norman Tolman.

Seaton Snooker League, Representative Team, late 1960s. These were the winners of the Bilby Devon Cup. Left to right: George Hoare (Colyton A), Alan Wellman (Lyme A), John Westbury (Chard A), Eddie Bonetta (Honiton A), Brian Wellman (Lyme A), Harold Parkhouse (Seaton A).

Axmouth United AFC, 1968/9 season. This team, competitors in the Perry Street League, Division 3, are in the car park of Axmouth Village Hall. They were League Champions, League Cup Winners and the Tommy Tabberer Cup Winners. Back row, left to right: Mike Clements, Phil Widger, Mike Long, Richard Hales, Melv Millman (captain), Alan Mitchell, Pete Perryman. Front row, left to right: Gerald Morgan, Keith Millman, Malcolm MacDonald, Terry Pavey, Richard Board.

Acknowledgements

I am grateful to all those people who, over the past forty years, have given photographs and postcards to add to my collection. My thanks go to Michael Clement of Axmouth, Albert Manley, Alan Parkman, Ross Dack and John Godfrey for loaning material for use in this book. Dick Iles of Colyton gave much help. These people have spoken from their own personal knowledge of times past and of their locality, so I would also like to thank all those who have contributed valuable information.

Thanks must go to Lyn Marshall, Norman Whinfrey, Roy Warburton and Geoff Sellers for much appreciated help. I am grateful to my wife, Carol, for all her help in this book, and to Simon Thraves for his assistance.

Although the dates presented are, in my opinion, correct, they could be up to ten years out.

Old photographs are truly fascinating. They bring back so vividly times past, and to live in them is never to die.